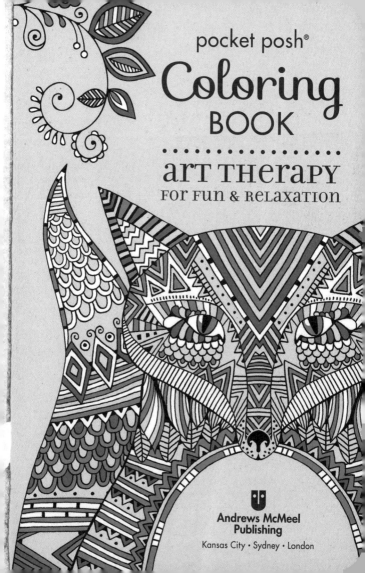

pocket posh®

Coloring
BOOK

• • • • • • • • • • • • • •

art THERAPY
FOR FUN & RELAXATION

Andrews McMeel
Publishing

Kansas City • Sydney • London

POCKET POSH® COLORING BOOK
art therapy for fun & relaxation

Andrews McMeel Publishing, LLC
an Andrews McMeel Universal company
1130 Walnut Street, Kansas City, Missouri 64106

www.andrewsmcmeel.com

15 16 17 18 SHZ 10 9 8 7 6 5 4 3 2

ISBN: 978-1-4494-5874-4

Illustrated by Hannah Davies, Richard Merritt, and Cindy Wilde
With additional material adapted from www.shutterstock.com

From doodling with loose lines and loops to coloring in complex designs, every activity in this book has been carefully crafted so you can enjoy the satisfaction of creating something beautiful.

With coloring and doodling, you need have no fear of making mistakes or failing. There is no right or wrong technique, only the opportunity to create stunning art. That's why this book contains no rules or complicated step-by-step instructions—you don't even have to stay within the lines if you don't want to.

From magical mandalas and rhythmical repeating patterns to gorgeous geometric designs and free-flowing doodles, the pictures in this book will help unlock your creativity and confidence. They will distract you from the stresses and strains of everyday life, and help you experience the calm that comes from focusing on simple tasks.

Pages for you to color are at the beginning of the book, and there are doodles to do at the back. So pick up a pen, choose a page you like the look of, and start drawing.

Coloring

Grab some pens or pencils and start coloring.
These drawings contain intricate sections that can
be filled in with a steady hand or scribbled over to
create an area of solid color.

Doodling

Find your coloring pens or pencils and finish off the following pages with lines, squiggles, and patterns. How you complete the drawings is entirely up to you—there are no rights or wrongs.

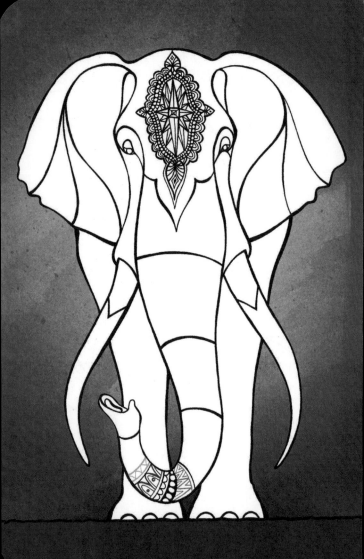

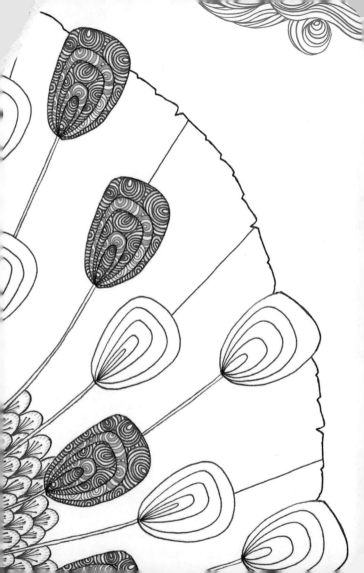

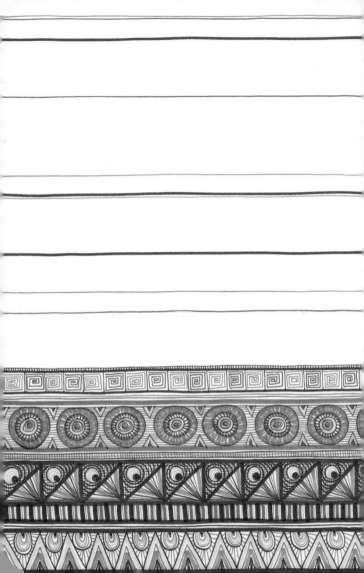

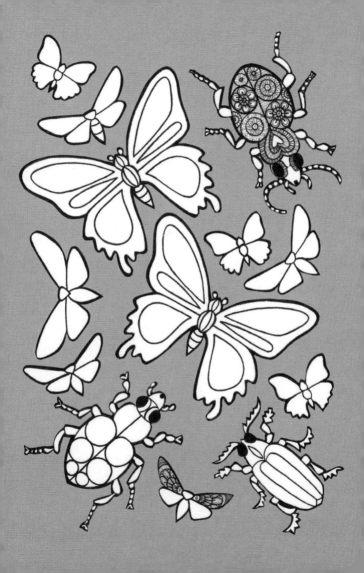